ENGLISH GRAMMAR
AND
WRITING MADE SIMPLE

Library of Congress Card Catalog Number: 2012919648

Brower, Wilbur L.

1. English Language—Grammar—Studying and teaching

Correspondence to the authors should be directed to:

Attn: Dr. Wilbur L. Brower
P. O. Box 565
Trenton, NC 28585

Phone: (910) 548-0698
E-mail: wlbrower@gmail.com

ISBN: 978-0-9884490-3-9

3

TABLE OF CONTENTS

==

We are what we repeatedly do.
Excellence, then, is not an act,
but a habit.

==

ARISTOTLE (384-422 B. C.)

Greek Mathematician & Philosopher

INTRODUCTION

English Grammar and Writing Made Simple is an outgrowth from frustrations I experienced working with students who need a much better **formal** understanding of the language they speak daily. While all of these students are highly communicative or verbal, many of them do not have a great facility with Standard *American* English and many are reading far below grade level. Therefore, the challenge for me was to develop learning processes for students to "attack" the language on a level that was within the bounds of their current skill level and to build upon their understanding of language, in general, to acquire a level of sophistication that they needed to do well as they progress through their studies and to do well on tests that purport to measure their linguistic abilities and verbal skills.

I also realized that this booklet would be an excellent primer for those who are learning English as a Second Language, or for those who learned to speak the language but did not acquire a sufficient under-standing of its *formal* structure.

The initial lesson starts with a simple two-word sentence, *Sasha barks*, and then adds other elements and features to demonstrate ways to change the character, complexity and intent of the sentence. Each element is explained and shows how it relates to the remainder or other elements of the sentence. The idea is to show how to a build sentence in order to build paragraphs in order to create more complex writings such as compositions, essays and novels. This is an incremental approach that does not overwhelm students, and it allows them to use and digest small chunks of the language and to incorporate it into their daily conversations. Examples are given with each concept or element, and students are encouraged to create their own examples to re-enforce the materials. I am convinced that this approach enhances their linguistic awareness and consciousness and changes their linguistic thinking and speaking habits.

Students will learn details about grammar and grammatical structures in context with sentence structures and purposes. This approach also allows them to understand the appropriate use of language to communicate intended messages, and it will help them to understand the inferences and subtleties associated with language.

By end of the booklet, students will have acquired a sufficient breadth and depth of understanding the language to write clear and concise sentences with the correct grammar, usage and mechanics. They will also have a greater curiosity about words and how they are used formally and informally.

This booklet, by no means, is intended to be the definitive publication on English Grammar and Composition, but it is a guide for learning the very basics of grammar and writing. The errors and omissions are those of the author.

HOW TO USE THIS BOOKLET

How do you learn a new poem, rap, song, a slang expression or popular words? Why do you learn them? People often learn things in order to fit in or to be popular among their peers. No matter why you learn things or what technique you use to learn them, it is a technique that you probably developed over time and it works for you. You can use that same technique to improve your understanding and use of the powerful information in this publication. It will serve you well throughout your educational experience and throughout your life.

This publication was designed primarily to be used in sequential order. This means that each concept or lesson is intended to build upon the previous one and eventually get you to the point where you have a very good understanding of Standard English and can write more accurately, clearly and concisely. You will note that it begins with basic elements of grammar, mechanics and usage and adds more complexity as the lessons unfold. I recommend that you find at least one-half hour each day to sit in your favorite study place and work on at least one concept or lesson. If you do not understand the concept or lesson the first time, go over it again and again until you do. Practice the concept or lesson and use it as many times as you can in your daily speaking and writings.

Take the work seriously, stay focused and see how powerful the results will be for you in your **reading, writing and speaking**.

Good Effort!

THE TRUTH ABOUT LANGUAGE

There are at least 6,800 different languages that are spoken in the world today, and we all are born with the innate capacity to speak every one of them. If we are immersed in an area where several languages are spoken, we will speak all of those languages as a matter of habit. To state it differently, we can learn to speak any language and to speak it very well. However, it is easier to learn a language when we first start learning to speak. So, our language, in essence, is a habit. We must **develop** writing and speaking habits that will help us, not hurt us. This takes time and effort, but it is achievable.

A language is made up of individual words that are put together to make or express a complete thought or an idea. There is *formal* language and *informal* language, often known as language registers. There is **no** good language or bad language. Language is the dominant or primary means of communicating, and it changes over time and can take on different meanings as it is used. Think about the language that is used in emails and text messages today and how it is being used to communicate. Although the structure of that "language" probably makes a lot of English teachers screech and scream, it is unlikely to stop anytime soon.

Formal language is used in formal communication, such as in business communications and learning situations. It is the language that is used in testing, and test-takers are expected to know it and to use it correctly.

Informal language is the language that is used in informal communication, such as when talking with family and friends. Informal language usually includes expressions or words that are not in common use. These expressions or words are known as dialect, idioms or slang.

Language typically mirrors the history and culture of its speakers. English speakers use words that have descended from earlier forms of English, French, Spanish and words borrowed from other languages.

Dialects often incorporate words or grammatical structures of other languages and Non-standard English. **Ebonics**, also known as Black English, is a combination of Standard English and West

African languages and includes an additional aspect indicating habitual action over time (*He be dancing*—he has been dancing for a while, not just now, and not just once). There are many dialects of English that are unique to various areas

Spanglish mixes both Spanish and English, and some elements of it can be found not only in the United States but in Latin America and Spain as well.

Regardless of how we choose to write and speak, we should be mindful that the way we write and speak can be an asset or a liability. An asset is something that will help us, and a liability is something that will hurt. It can be a passport to many great opportunities. We often deny ourselves those opportunities because we have *elected* not to learn to write and speak Standard English. We've made a choice, or we've failed to put in the effort to do it. Either way, people make judgments about us based on the way we write and speak. If we do not have a good command of the language, they assume that we are illiterate and unintelligent, regardless of our intellectual abilities.

Remember that verbal and written communication with Standard English is a highly valued commodity in business and educational settings and formal interpersonal interactions. Choose to do it well.

BUILDING SENTENCES

Sentences are words that express a complete thought or idea, or several complete thoughts or ideas. A complete sentence always tells *who* or *what* and *what* is or what happens. Sentences can range in length from very short to very long.

Example: Sasha barks.

This is a **simple sentence**. It has a **subject** and a **predicate** or **verb.**

The subject of a sentence identifies someone or something that is being talked about: **Sasha**

The **predicate** or **verb** tells what the subject is or is doing: **barks**

We can add words to a simple sentence to give it "color" or character. They tell additional information about the subject and verb. These words are **adjectives, adverbs** and **prepositions**.

An **adjective** is a word that modifies, describes or gives additional information about some part of the discussion.

17

Adjectives describe nouns by answering one of these questions: *What kind is it? How many are there? Which one is it?* An adjective can be a single word, a phrase, or a clause.(More about that later.)

     Example: **Little** Sasha barks.

We've added an adjective to describe or give additional information about Sasha. We could have added two words, such as **sweet little** to give additional information about Sasha.

Most **adverbs** tell us how, where, when or why something is done. In other words, they describe the manner, place, or time of an action. They tell more about a verb in a sentence.

     Example: Little Sasha barks **loudly.**

Loudly tells **how** Sasha barks.

Adverbs can also modify or give additional information about another adverb.

     Example: Little Sasha barks **loudly every morning**.

This sentence tells **how** Sasha barks and **when** she barks.

Most, **but not all**, adverbs end in –**ly**. Most of these are created by adding -**ly** to the end of an adjective.

A preposition introduces a noun or pronoun or a phrase or clause functioning in the sentence as a noun. The word or word group that the preposition introduces is its **object**. A preposition links nouns, pronouns and phrases to other words in a sentence. A preposition usually indicates the temporal (time), spatial or logical relationship of its object to the rest of the sentence.

Example: Little Sasha barks loudly every morning
from her bed.

The word or phrase that the preposition introduces is called the **object of the preposition**.

The most common prepositions: about, above, across, after, against, along, among, around, at, before, behind, below, beneath, beside, between, beyond, but, by, despite, down, during, except, for, from, in, inside, into, like, near, of, off, on, onto, out, outside, over, past, since, through, throughout, till, to, toward, under, underneath, until, up, upon, with, within, and without.

A conjunction is a word that links words, phrases, or clauses. The word **and** connects the two independent clauses.

Example: Little Sasha barks loudly every morning **from** her bed, **and** then she jumps on the floor.

Example: Little Sasha barks loudly every morning **from** her bed. Then she jumps on the floor.

Sentences can include **clauses** and **phrases.**

A clause is a group of related words containing a **subject** and a **verb**. It is different from a **phrase**.

A phrase is a group of words that acts in a sentence as a single part of speech. A phrase **does not** include a subject and a verb relationship.

Examples: One of my favorite meals is duck **under glass**. (modifies the noun duck)

The little piper cub sputtered **into the sky**. (modifies the verb sputtered)

An Independent clause can stand by itself and still make sense. An independent clause could be its own sentence, but is often part of a larger structure, combined with other independent clauses and with dependent clauses. Independent clauses are sometimes called **essential** or **restrictive** clauses.

Independent clauses can be connected in a variety of ways:

1. By a comma and little **conjunction** (*for, and, nor, but, or, yet,* and sometimes *so. The first letter of each of these words is an acronym for FANBOYS).*

2. By a semicolon, by itself.

3. By a semicolon accompanied by a conjunctive adverb (such as *however, moreover, nevertheless, as a result, consequently,* etc.).

4. And, of course, independent clauses are often not connected by a punctuation at all, but are separated by a period.

A **Dependent** clause **cannot** stand by itself. It depends on something else, an independent clause, for its meaning. A dependent clause trying to stand by itself would be a **sentence fragment.** Dependent clauses are sometimes called **subordinate, nonessential,** or **nonrestrictive** clauses.

The **dependent clause** begins with what is called a subordinating conjunction. This causes the clause to be dependent upon the rest of the sentence for it to make sense; it cannot stand by itself.

Dependent clauses can be identified and classified according to their role in the sentence.

Adverb Clauses tend to tell us something about the sentence's main verb: when, why, under what conditions.

Adjective Clauses modify nouns or pronouns in the rest of the sentence.

A Complex Sentence has an **independent clause** and one or more **dependent/subordinate clauses**.

Examples: <u>**When** little Sasha barks loudly every morning from her bed and jumps on the floor,</u> I know it is time to get up.

<u>**When** little Sasha barks loudly every morning from her bed and jumps on the floor,</u> I know it is time to get up and let her out for a walk.

<u>**After** Sasha finishes her walk,</u> she is ready to sleep

Notice how the dependent clauses begin with "dependent words," which are words that **subordinate** what follows to the rest of the sentence. These words are also called **subordinating conjunctions,** and include **because, before, although, after, because, unless, since, whenever, while,** etc. These words do not usually introduce a complete thought. The clause requires additional information, a complete sentence, to make sense.

Notice how the **subject** is often separated from its **verb** by information represented by the dependent clause.

Examples: Sasha, **who was rescued from an animal shelter**, is a little Pomeranian puppy.

The puppy **that was rescued from an animal shelter** is a Pomeranian.

Intervening Prepositional Phrases usually separate the subject from its verb. This often causes confusion about the subject and verb agreement.

Example: The rhythm **of the rushing waves** was soothing.

The subject of the sentence is **rhythm,** which is singular, and the prepositional phrase, of course, is **of the rushing waves.** The correct verb is was, which is singular for the singular subject **rhythm.**

CONDITIONAL SENTENCES AND INTRODUCTORY CLAUSES

Conditional Sentences are also known as Conditional Clauses, If Clauses or Zero Condition Sentence. They are used to express that the action in the main clause (without *if*) can only take place if a certain condition (in the clause with *if*) is fulfilled. An **"if" clause** and a **main clause** will mean the same thing if **"when"** is used instead of **"if."**

It is possible and also very likely that the condition will be fulfilled.

Example: **If I find her address**, I'll send her an invitation.

The main clause can also be at the beginning of the sentence. In this case, don't use a comma.

Example: I will send her an invitation if I find her address.

Note: The main clause and/or **if clause** might be negative.

> Example: If I don't see Neil this afternoon, I will phone him in the evening.

Introductory Clauses

Introductory clauses are dependent clauses that provide background information or "set the stage" for the main part of the sentence, the independent clause.

> Examples: **If they want to win,** athletes must exercise every day. (introductory dependent clause, main clause)
>
> **Because she kept barking insistently,** we threw the ball for Sasha. (introductory dependent clause, main clause)

Clue: Introductory clauses start with adverbs: *after, although, as, because, before, if, since, though, until, when,* etc.

KINDS/PURPOSES OF SENTENCES

There are four (4) kinds of sentences that serve four specific purposes:

Declarative—A declarative sentence **makes a statement.** A declarative sentence ends with a period.

    Example: The house will be built on a hill.

Interrogative—An interrogative sentence **asks a question.** An interrogative sentence ends with a question mark.

    Example: How did you find the house?

Exclamatory—An exclamatory sentence **shows strong feeling.** An exclamatory sentence ends with an exclamation mark.

    Example: The monster is attacking!

Imperative—An imperative sentence **gives a command.** An imperative sentence ends with a period.

    Example: Travis, close the door.

Sometimes the subject of an imperative sentence (you) is understood.

    Example: Look in the closet. (You, look in the closet.)

Note that the punctuation mark at the end of a sentence can tell what kind of sentence it is.

SENTENCE STRUCTURES

There are four sentence structures: **Simple, Compound, Complex and Compound-Complex.**

Simple Sentence—A simple sentence has one independent clause. It is the basic subject/verb statement.

   Example: Sasha walked yesterday.

Compound Sentence—A compound sentence has two independent clauses joined by a comma and a coordinating conjunction [for, and, nor, but, or, yet, so (FANBOYS)] or a semi-colon (;). Each independent clause is a complete sentence and can stand alone.

   Examples: Sasha walked yesterday, and she will walk again tomorrow.

             Sasha walked yesterday; she will walk again tomorrow.

Complex Sentence—A complex sentence has an independent clause and one or more dependent/subordinate clauses. Dependent/subordinate clauses cannot stand alone.

27

Example: Although Sasha walked yesterday, she needs to walk again tomorrow.

Much of the complex sentence's effectiveness comes from the power of the subordinating adverb (because, although, after, etc.). Dependent clauses usually appear at the beginning or/and at the end of complex sentences.

Examples: After Sasha walked yesterday, she was ready to eat.

Sasha was ready to eat after she walked yesterday.

Do not use a comma if the dependent clause comes at the end of the sentence.

Compound-Complex Sentence—A compound-complex sentence has one or more independent clauses and one or more subordinate clauses.

Example: After Sasha walked yesterday, she was ready to eat, and she was ready to go to sleep.

SENTENCE FRAGMENTS AND RUN-ON SENTENCES

A Sentence Fragment is an incomplete sentence. It is a part of a sentence that has been punctuated as if it were a complete sentence. Often, it is missing a **subject, verb or part of a verb string.**

A sentence without a stated or implied subject is incomplete.

Example: Shortly after his birth, was baptized in a small church in Goldsboro, NC.

The fragment does not tell **who** was baptized in a small church in Goldsboro, NC.

A sentence without a verb or a complete verb does not tell the reader the exact message the writer is trying to send.

Example: Diandre´ working hard on his class project lately.

In this case, the auxiliary or helping verb has been is the only logical one that's missing and would complete the verb string and the sentence.

A sentence fragment can give a lot of information and still not be a complete sentence:

Example: After the teacher encouraged her so much last year
           and she seemed
           to improve each week.

There, in fact, are two subject and verb relationships in the sentence (*teacher encouraged* and *she seemed*), but the entire clause is subordinate by the dependent word *after*. We need an independent clause to complete the sentence.

A sentence fragment can have a string of prepositional phrases that never get around to establishing a subject and verb relationship to complete the sentence.

Example: Immediately **after building Dillard School**
           and **during the early years** as the predominant
           educational institution **for Blacks in Goldsboro.**

Be careful of sentence fragments that give their share of information but still don't contain a subject and verb.

Run-on sentences are two or more complete sentences that run together as if they were one complete sentence. There are two types of run-on sentences:

1. Fused sentence—has no punctuation between the complete sentences.

   Example: Della sold her hair to buy Jim a chain for his watch
   Jim sold his watch to buy Della combs for her hair.

2. Comma splice—has only a comma between the complete sentences.

   Example: Della sold her hair to buy Jim a chain for his watch;
   Jim sold his watch to buy Della combs for her hair.

There are five (5) ways to correct a run-on sentence:

– Make two sentences.
– Use a comma and a coordinating conjunction.
– Use a semicolon.
– Use a semicolon and a conjunctive adverb. (therefore, instead, still, also, however, moreover, consequently, etc.).
– Change one of the complete thoughts into a subordinate clause.

Make two sentences.
   Example: Della sold her hair to buy Jim a chain for his watch.

Jim sold his watch to buy Della combs for her hair.

Use a comma and a coordinating conjunction.

> Example: Della sold her hair to buy Jim a chain for his watch, **and** Jim sold his watch to buy Della combs for her hair.

Use a semicolon.

> Example: Della sold her hair to buy Jim a chain for his watch; Jim sold his watch to buy Della combs for her hair.

Use a semicolon and a conjunctive adverb

> Example: Della sold her hair to buy Jim a chain for his watch; **however** Jim sold his watch to buy Della combs for her hair.

Change one of the complete thoughts into a subordinate clause.

> Example: **After** Della sold her hair to but Jim a chain for his watch, Jim sold his watch to buy Della combs for her hair.

The word **after** introduces a dependent or subordinate clause and needs the **independen**t clause, *Jim sold his watch to buy Della combs for her hair,* to make a complete sentence.

PERFECTING SENTENCES

Writing the perfect sentence requires thought, first about what you want to say, and then how best to say it. Many sentences or combinations of sentences can be improved by using a few simple techniques. These techniques include **compounding, coordinating and varying sentences, inserting words** and **reducing and subordinating clauses.** While these techniques might not produce the perfect sentence, they will improve its overall flow and readability. Perfecting sentences is usually done during the editing stage of your writing process. It allows you to see that sentences can be flexible in how they convey your ideas and thoughts. The more practice you have perfecting sentences the better you will become.

Compounding Sentences involves combining simple sentences that have the same subjects or verbs. This results in one sentence with a compound subject or a compound verb.

Examples: Jay´Quan likes basketball. I like basketball, too.

Jay´Quan and **I** like basketball.

33

We went to The Lighthouse. We had ice-cream at The Lighthouse.

We **went** to The Lighthouse and **had** ice-cream.

Coordinating Sentences involves using coordinating conjunctions or correlative conjunctions (both…and; not only…but; either…or; neither…nor; whether…or) to form simple sentences into compound sentences.

Examples: Ke Juan in only fifteen. He is a terrific ballplayer.

Ke Juan is only fifteen, **but** he is a terrific ballplayer.

Carpentry work is not all we do. We also paint.

We **not only** do carpentry work **but** also paint.

Inserting Words and Phrases

Examples: A book was left behind. It was under a desk.

A book was left behind **under the desk**.

The soup was thick. It was flavorful.

The **flavorful** soup was thick.

Varying Sentences can clarify the relationship and the importance of ideas. It can also give your work variety and show contrast.

Examples: We walked to school. The day was warm.

We walked to school, **for** the day was warm.

English met at in the morning. Gym met after lunch.

English met at noon, **and** Gym met after lunch.

Reducing Clauses can result in only a few words.

Example: Because she was discouraged about her writing, Diamond decided to try acting.

Discouraged by her writing, Diamond decided to try acting.

A Subordinating Clause allows you to emphasize an independent clause. It also allows you to add sentence variety to your writing.

Example: It began to snow. Tarius headed for the ski slopes.

When it began to snow, Tarius headed for the ski slopes.

PUNCTUATIONS

Punctuation marks dictate the flow of ideas and thoughts in a sentence. They are similar to a traffic cop who, in order to ensure an orderly flow, controls the traffic as it makes its way through a busy city street. Punctuation marks are used to help the reader to decipher accurately the message a written passage contains. In other words, the essential purpose of punctuation marks is to clarify ideas and thoughts. If punctuation marks are used *incorrectly*, the written passage may contain *inaccurate* or *unintended* messages.

Different punctuation marks serve different purposes. Some separate ideas and words; others place emphases on ideas and words; yet, others categorize and group together related ideas and words, or ensure that they remain together. Without clear punctuation marks, written materials would be confusing or misleading.

Rules for punctuation are easy to understand and apply, but first they must be learned and used in ways they are intended, not in ways the writer chooses to use them or is accustomed to using them. This section will explain how to use the more common punctuations that writers are likely to encounter in everyday usage.

The Comma (,)—is the most misused of all punctuation marks and accounts for more than half of all punctuation errors. Therefore, more space will be dedicated to this punctuation challenge. The following rules demonstrate how to punctuate more clearly and effectively to ensure that accurate and intended passages are contained in written materials.

Use the comma to set off:

> **Independent or main clauses**—A comma follows the first of **two independent clauses** that are joined by coordinating conjunctions (for, and, nor, but, or, yet, and so):

The story's main character is Sasha, **and** its author is Sy Oliver.

Oliver's early stories were more popular, **but** his later ones have failed.

Note that the comma comes **before** the conjunction.

Do not use a comma if there is not a full clause after the conjunction.

Wrong: Sasha barked loudly, and jumped on her bed.

Right: Sasha barked loudly and jumped on her bed.

Items in a series—Use commas to separate clauses, phrases and words in a series of three or more.

Examples:

Clauses: Carol took Spanish classes, she studied cooking, and she worked a part-time job.

Phrases: The video is available in the media center, in the classroom and at the video rental shop.

Words: I enjoy the writings of Steinbeck, Cooper, Grisham, and Hemingway.

Introductory Devices—Use commas to introduce:

An introductory adverb clause:

Example: **If you pay my cell phone bill today,** I'll repay you tomorrow.

A long prepositional phrase:

Example: **In the middle of a hot summer day**, we went for a long walk along the beach.

Parenthetical Phrases—or expressions are words or groups of words that interrupt the main flow, idea or thought of a sentence.

While parenthetical expressions are not essential to the meaning of the sentence, they provide additional information about it. There are several types of parenthetical expressions.

Examples: This book report, **in my opinion,** is one of the best.

This book report, **on the other hand,** is not too bad.

A Nonrestrictive or Nonessential Clause is parenthetical. This clause gives information that is not essential to the meaning of the sentence.

Therefore, you may omit or take out the clause and still get the meaning of sentence. The parenthetical clause is set off with comma.

Examples: Herman Street, **which runs alongside the school,** is always busy.

The coach, who attended Mt. Olive College, won the first State Championship for the school.

A restrictive clause is important to the meaning of the sentence. It gives additional information about a preceding noun in the sentence and answers the question "which one?" Restrictive clauses are not set off by commas.

39

Examples: The car **that she bought** was recalled.

The man **who lives next door** is an Air Force veteran.

Without these clauses, the sentences could refer to any car or any man.

A Nonrestrictive or Nonessential Phrase—This phrase gives information that is not essential to meaning of the sentence. Therefore, you may omit or take out the phrase and still get the meaning of the sentence. The parenthetical phrase is set off with comma.

Examples: Cynthia, **wearing a red scarf**, is Sheila's best friend.

The S-500 Mercedes, **with the red bow,** is her birthday gift.

Coordinate Adjectives—In a series of two or more, use commas to separate adjectives of equal value or importance. Do not use a comma after the last adjective in the series.

Examples: The **tall, statuesque** woman over there is a model.
Crude, profane or vulgar language is not tolerated

here.

Names and Other Words Used in Direct Address:

Examples: Aaron, when are you going to Atlanta?

For my senior project, Mr. Patrick, I'm producing a DVD.

Yes or No at the Beginning of a Sentence:
Examples: No, I don't expect to attend the ceremony.

Yes, I am leaving for Chicago early tomorrow morning.

Direct Quotations—Use commas to separate a direct quote from the preceding or following words.
Examples: "I'm not going to take it anymore," she said.

"Of all days," she said, "you had to come home today without your iPod"

Before a Confirmatory Question:
Examples: It's about time to go, **isn't it?**

You're not leaving now, **are you?**

The Period (.) is used at the end of every sentence except a **direct** question or an exclamation.

Examples: We will have the quiz next Friday.

I asked how I could buy oranges for a good price. (This is an **indirect** question. The direct question

41

would be: How can I buy oranges for a good price?)

After a Non-sentence

Examples: Good Afternoon.

Good Morning.

The Semicolon (;) indicates that there is a greater break in a thought than the comma but a lesser break than the period. The semicolon is often interchangeable with the period.

Between Independent Clauses Not Joined by a Coordinating Conjunction

Example: World War I was rough; World War II was rougher.

Between Independent Clauses Joined by a Conjunctive Adverb (*also, besides, consequently; furthermore, however, in fact; likewise, meanwhile, nevertheless; otherwise, still, therefore; then and thus*).

Examples: The store was closed; however, the manager let us in.

It's getting late; therefore, I must leave.

Between Items in a Series When There Are Commas within the Items—Add a semicolon after every three items in the series.

Example: We had chicken, rice, string beans; corn, potato salad; biscuits, cornbread, banana pudding; chocolate cake, ice-cream and iced-tea.

The Colon (:) is used to introduce:

A List of Something or Things That Follow:

Examples: You received the award for one reason: your scholarship.

The first team consists of four sophomores: Baker, Darden, Jackson and Thompson.

A Long Quotation (usually one or more paragraphs):

Example: In the beginning of novel <u>Uncle Tom's Cabin</u>, Harriet Beecher Stow wrote:

Late in the afternoon on a chilly day in February, two gentlemen were sitting alone over their wine, in a well-furnished dining parlor, in the town of P____, in Kentucky. There were no servants present, and the gentlemen, with chairs closely approaching, seemed to be discussing some subject with great earnestness.

When quotations are introduced by a colon, it is unnecessary to surround them with quotations marks.

The Question Mark (?) is used:
After a Direct Question

Example: Where are you going?

What time is it?

You're not leaving now, are you?

Within Parentheses to Indicate Doubt or Uncertainty

Example: The school opened in 1954 (?) and closed in 2004.

The Apostrophe (') is used to:

Form the Possessive Case of Singular and Plural Nouns

Examples: This is the boy's coat.

These are the boys' coats.

The woman's dress is here.

The women's dresses are here.

Show Contractions and Other Omission of Letters or Numerals

Examples: don't (do not)

who's (who is)

class of '85 (1985)

For the Plurals of Letters, Numbers, Symbols and Words

Examples: She made all A's.

He uses too many and's in his writings.

His career peaked in the 1980's.

The Exclamation Point (!) Is Used After an Emphatic Word, Sentence or Other Expression.

Examples: What a shot!

Fantastic!

I can't believe she got that scholarship!

The Parenthesis [( )] is used to:

Set Off Incidental Information:

Examples: Senator Elizabeth Dole (R., NC) will leave the U. S. Congress in January 2009.

Enclose references, numbers and questions marks:

Examples: The picture (see page 125) is very beautiful.

She has authority to (1) tutor, (2) impose discipline, and (3) check notebooks.

The school opened in 1954 (?) and closed in 2004.

The Hyphen is used to:

Join Certain Compound Words:

Examples: brother-in-law

Hop-scotch

Attorneys-at-Law

Sergeant-at-Arms

Join Words Used as a Single Adjective before a Noun:

Examples: Herman is a well-traveled street.

He is a much-admired student.

Write Two-Word Numbers from 21-99 and Two-Word Fractions:

Examples: twenty-five   two-thirds

Sixty-first   Three-fourths

Introduce the Prefixes *ex* and *self*, and the suffix *elect*:

Examples: Bill Clinton is an ex-president.

She has a lot of self-confidence.

President-elect Obama will be sworn in January 20, 2009.

Divide a Word That Will Not Fit at the End of a Sentence:

Examples: The classroom is too small to **accommodate** all
the students.

That requires us to have a **temporary staging
area**.

The hyphen has to be placed between two syllables.

NOUNS

A **Noun** is a word that names an idea, person, place or thing. Anything that exists can be named, and that name is a noun. Nouns are divided generally into several categories or types.

An **Abstract Noun** You cannot *see* them, *hear* them, *smell* them, *taste* them, or *feel* them

Examples:	Bravery	Confidence
	Intelligence	Loyalty
	Sadness	Temperature

A **Collective Noun** names groups [*things*] composed of *members* [usually *people*].

Examples:	company	team
	jury	committee
	audience	band

A Common Noun is not capitalized and it refers to any person, place or thing.

Examples:	Boy	Girl
	Desk	Computer

A **Concrete Noun**-- You can experience this group of nouns with your five senses: you *see* them, *hear* them, *smell* them, *taste* them, and *feel* them.

Examples: Car   Baseball

Jacket   Dog

Tooth   Toy

A **Count Noun** can have both a singular and plural form. If you **can add** a **number** to the front of a noun and put an s at the end of it, you have a count noun.

Examples: Cookie   Cookies

Chair   Chairs

Book   Books

A **Non-Count** Noun is a noun you **cannot add** a **number** to the front or an s to the end of.

Examples: Furniture   Homework

Information   Weather

A **Proper Noun** names a **specific** person, place, or thing

Examples: Cairo   Catholicism

Democratic Party   God

49

Malaysia   Middle East

Queen Cynthia   Unitarianism

Proper Nouns are **always** capitalized.

A **Compound Noun** is made of two or more words. Compound Nouns may be **open, hyphenated or closed**:

Examples: Line of sight (open)

Sergeant-at-arms (hyphenated)

Postmaster (closed)

Number of a noun refers to whether it is either singular or plural. However, there are some nouns that are either singular or plural, depending upon the context of the sentence in which they are used. A plural form of a noun names more than one thing. To form the plural of most nouns, simply add **-s.** For nouns ending in **s, ch, sh, x**, or z, add–**es.**

Singular   Plural

Examples: church   churches
    box   boxes

For nouns ending in **y** preceded by a consonant, change **y** to **i** and add –**es**.

	Singular	Plural
Examples	mystery	mysteries
	story	stories

For most nouns ending in **f** or **fe**, change the **f** to **v** and add –**es**.

	Singular	Plural
Examples:	shelf	shelves
	knife	knives
	wolf	wolves

Some nouns have **irregular** plural forms.

	Singular	Plural
Examples:	woman	women
	child	children
	goose	geese
	tooth	teeth

Some nouns do not change form from singular to plural.

	Singular	Plural
Examples:	deer	deer
	sheep	sheep
	fish	fish

The possessive form of a noun shows possession, ownership or relationship between two nouns. Add an apostrophe (') and an –**s** to form the possessive of any singular noun. Use an apostrophe (') only to form the possessive of a plural that ends in s.

	Singular	Plural
Examples:	cat's toy	cats' toy
	wife's car	wives' cars
	baby's bottle	babies' bottles

VERBS AND VERB FORMS

The verb is the essential part of every sentence. The verb tells the time an action or an event occurred. It tells what the subject does (did or will do), or that subject is (was or will be) something. Unless a sentence has a verb, it is only a fragment of a sentence and not a complete sentence. A sentence may contain only one word, but it must be the verb.

Examples: Stop!

Run.

Every verb must have a subject. In the examples above, it is understood that the word "you" is the subject.

Identifying the verb is an easy process. The verb is the word that will usually change its form if you change the time of the event in the sentence

We usually determine from the verb whether an action or event is happening now, happened in the past, or is at some other time. The **present, past** and **past particle** verb forms are used most frequently. Verb forms are called **tense**. Putting verbs in their proper tenses is called **conjugation.**

TENSES:

Present Tense

When we speak of something that is happening now, we use the present tense.

Add an "s," or "ies" to the verb for **third person singular** subjects.

First person—I hear.

Second Person—You hear.

Third Person—He, she or it hears.
He, she or it **tries**.

The present tense also can use the "ing" ending.

She is <u>walking.</u>

Past Tense

When we speak of something that happened in the past, we use the past tense.

To form the past tense of **regular verbs**, we merely add "d" or "ed" to the present tense. In some instances for verbs that end in

54

the letter "y," change the "y" to the letter "I" and add "ed."

1)   I <u>heard</u>.
2)   You <u>whistled.</u>
3)   He, she, it <u>whistled.</u>
4)   I've <u>tried</u> that trick before.

NOTE: **Irregular verb** tenses usually change form—
Discussed later.

1)   He <u>went</u> to the store.

Past Participle

The past participle is another form of past. It uses the "helper" verb. When using a regular verb, take the past form of it and add a "helper" verb to form the past participle.

1)   I <u>have</u> heard that story many times.

2)   She <u>has</u> danced her way to the championship.

In order to understand tense easier, it is important to know the meaning of a **regular verb** and an **irregular verb.**

A **regular verb** is one that goes from present, past to past participle while keeping/retaining the root word.

	Present	**Past**	**Past Participle**
Example:	walk	walked	have walked

Notice that the word *walk* is kept/retained with each verb tense.

An irregular verb is one that changes form when it is conjugated.

	Present	**Past**	**Past Participle**
Examples:	go	went	have gone

Notice that there is no trace of the initial word, *go*, in the past and past participle verb tenses. The past participles of irregular verbs cause the greatest challenge for most students. These verb forms must be studied carefully and remembered. Also, remember that the past participle form of any verb requires the use of an auxiliary or helping verb. A list of **Irregular Verbs** and their **Present, Past and Past Participle Tenses,** along with other verb conjugations, is included in the Appendix of this booklet.

In some instances, the verb form does not change from the present, past and past participle tenses:

	Present	**Past**	**Past Participle**
Examples:	cut	cut	have cut

| quit | quit | have quit |
| cost | cost | has cost |

An **Auxiliary Verb** is a **Supplemental Verb** that is "helping" the main verb. The common auxiliary or helping verbs are:

TO BE: is, am, are, was, were, been

TO DO: do, did, does

TO HAVE: has, had, have

SHALL, WILL, MAY, CAN, SHOULD, COULD, WOULD

Verbs have forms known as **infinitives, participles and gerunds. These are called verbals, but they act as nouns, adjectives and adverbs.**

The **infinitive** is introduced with the word "to" plus the verb.

Examples: Noun—**To talk** now is useless. (subject)

Adjective—This is the book **to read**. (modifies book)

Adverb—She came to **help.** (modifies came)

The **participle** can be **present** or **past** and is used as an **adjective**. The **present participle** is the verb plus "ing."

Example: The **burning** car caught my attention.

The suv, **swaying** wildly, finally flipped. (modifies suv)

The **past participle** is the verb plus "ed" for regular and "en" or another irregular verb ending.

Examples: The burned chicken was all thrown out. (modifies chicken)

Stricken with fear, the team put off their regular practice. (modifies team)

The Verb Forms Table below gives a more complete picture of the conjugation of a few sample verbs.

INFINITIVE	BASE/SIMPLE	PAST	PRESENT PARTICIPLE	PAST PARTICIPLE
To finish	Finish	Finished	Finishing	Finished
To swim	Swim	Swam	Swimming	Swum

58

To buy	Buy	Bought	Buying	Bought
To go	Go	Went	Going	Gone
To sit	Sit	Sat	Sitting	Sat
To drive	Drive	Drove	Driving	Driven
To speak	Speak	Spoke	Speaking	Spoken
To talk	Talk	Talked	Talking	Talked
To bring	Bring	Brought	Bringing	Brought

Always use a helping verb (have, has, had, could have, should have, was, were, etc.) with past participle verb forms

59

SUBJECT AND VERB AGREEMENT

While there are approximately twenty (20) rules for verb and subject agreements, the most important rule is that the verb must agree with the intended number of the subject. This means that if you have a subject that is **singular (one** person, place or thing), you have to have a **singular verb.** Conversely, if you have a subject that is **plural (more than one** person, place or thing), you must use a **plural verb.** Once you have a basic understanding of subject and verb agreement, rules that are more complex become easier to figure out. Only a few of the rules will be mentioned here. To begin the understanding, follow two occasionally not-so-simple tasks:

1. Identify the real subject

2. Determine whether the subject is singular or plural

This can be a challenge in cases in which long clauses with extensive phrases can make proper subject verb agreement more difficult to identify. The first step is often made difficult by phrases and/or sentence structures that make it difficult to identify the true subject of the sentence. The prepositional phrase is one of the main culprits

60

that cause the misidentification of the true subject of the clause.

Examples: The **colors** of the rainbow **fascinate** me.

The **color** of the rainbow **fascinates** me.

The word "colors" in the first example is the subject, "fascinate" is the verb, and "of the rainbow" is the prepositional phrase. The word "color" in the first example is the subject, and "fascinates" is the verb, and "of the rainbow" is the prepositional phrase. In each example, the subjects and verbs agree in number.

Prepositional phrases between the subject and verb usually do not affect agreement.

Parenthetical phrases can also work to obscure the true subject. Phrases such as "as well as," "such as," "along with," "rather than," "accompanied by" and "including" introduce items that are NOT considered when determining whether a verb is singular or plural.

Examples: **He**, along with the other fathers, **is** going to see the Charlotte Bobcats play Saturday night.

The **textbook**, in addition to supplementary materials, is on the table next to the window.

The men's basketball **coaches**, as well as the cheerleaders' coach, **were** given citizen ship awards.

Words, commonly known as sentence interrupters, that come between the subject and verb should not affect agreement.

If two subjects in a sentence are joined by *and*, they typically require a plural verb form.

Example: The cat **and** the dog **are going** to the Vet tomorrow.

The verb is singular if the two subjects separated by *and* refer to the same person or thing.

Example: Ice-cream and cookies **is** Cynthia's favorite **dish**.

Collective nouns like herd, senate, class, crowd, etc. usually take a singular verb form.

Example: The *herd* is stampeding.

Titles of books, movies, novels, etc. are treated as singular and take a singular verb.

Example: *The Thorns Birds* is a great series.

PRONOUNS

Pronouns are words used in the place of a noun and they share almost all the uses of nouns. The main kinds of pronouns are: Personal, Interrogative and Relative. Pronouns are used in three situations.

First Person— They may refer to the person speaking.

I raised *my* hand.

We will go.

That flashlight is *mine*.

Second Person— They may refer to someone spoken to.

Have *you* forgotten *your* gloves.

Are the notebooks *yours?*

Third Person— They may refer to other persons, places, and things.

Chris reached for the paper, but *it* floated away.

The boys are looking for *him*.

Sagina says that book is *hers.*

She spoke to *him* yesterday.

They brought *their* cameras with *them.*

From these examples, we see that a pronoun often refers to a person. The largest group of pronouns is called personal pronouns, and they are classified by cases, which are **Nominative, Objective and Possessive.**

Nouns and pronouns in English are said to display *case* according to their function in the sentence. They can be **subjective** or **nominative** (which means they act as the subject of independent or dependent clauses), **possessive** (which means they show possession of something else), or **objective** (which means they function as the recipient of action or are the object of a preposition). The following table outlines the cases and numbers (singular and plural) of the personal pronouns:

THE PERSONAL PRONOUNS—SINGULAR

CASE:	NOMINATIVE/ SUBJECTIVE	OBJECTIVE	POSSESSIVE
FIRST PERSON	I	Me	My, mine
SECOND PERSON	You	You	Your, yours
THIRD PERSON	He, she, it	Him, her, it	His, hers, its

THE PERSON PRONOUND—PLURAL

CASE:	NOMINATIVE/ SUBJECTIVE	OBJECTIVE	POSSESSIVE
FIRST PERSON	We	Us	Our, ours
SECOND PERSON	You	You	Your, yours
THIRD PERSON	They	Them	Theirs

Pronouns have to agree with the subjects they replace. Plural subjects must have plural pronouns, and singular subjects must have singular pronouns.

Examples: **Incorrect:** If a boy wants to impress a girl, <u>they</u> better do more than look at her.

Correct: If a boy wants to impress a girl, <u>he</u> better do more than look at her.

Incorrect: When someone is lonely, <u>they </u>usually go on a picnic.

Correct: When someone is lonely, <u>he or she</u> usually goes on a picnic.

Interrogative Pronouns ask a question. They are: Who (whose, whom), which and what.

Examples: Whose book is that?

Which of those hats is his?

Who spoke those words?

Relative Pronouns are the same as interrogative pronouns, plus **that** and the –**ever** forms: whoever, whomever, whichever and whatever. The relative pronouns introduce certain kinds of dependent clauses, sometimes called relative clauses.

Examples: The girl **who called** was upset.

Charlotte, **which is a great city,** is an exciting place to visit.

INDEFINITE PRONOUNS

Some **Indefinite Pronouns** are **always singular, some are always plural** and **some are bimodal,** which means they may be either singular or plural. All third person indefinite pronouns are singular and require a singular verb:

any**one**	any**body**	any**thing**
every**one**	every**body**	every**thing**
some**one**	some**body**	some**thing**
no **one**	no**body**	nothing
each	every	one
either	neither	another
other	much	

Examples: **Everybody is** going except you.

Is anyone coming to relieve me?

Anything you choose to do is fine with me.

Either of them **is** sufficient.

Each of the boys **is** coming home today.

Nothing they do **is** going to be satisfactory.

67

Plural Indefinite Pronouns take plural verbs:

Both of the boys **are** home for Christmas.

Few are likely to be early.

Many things **are** on the agenda.

Several friends **are** coming over to celebrate the New Year.

Bimodal Indefinite Pronouns can take either the singular or plural verb. These pronouns:

More	any	some	half
most	**a**ll	**n**one	

These indefinite pronouns create the acronym **MASHMAN**.

To determine the subject and verb agreement, look at the prepositional phrase that follows those bimodal indefinite pronouns. If the object of the preposition is singular, the pronoun takes a singular subject. If the object of the preposition is plural, the pronoun takes a plural subject.

Examples: **Most** of the **books are** new.

Most of the **sky is** blue.

None of the **DVDs have** been returned.

None of the **paint is** left.

ADJECTIVES AND ADVERBS

Adjectives are words that describe or modify a person or thing in the sentence. The articles *a, an,* and *the* are adjectives. Adjectives are positive, comparative or superlative. Comparative and superlatives show degrees of comparisons.

Comparative and superlatives forms of adjectives are used to compare two or more things. Generally, comparatives are formed using **-er** and superlatives are formed using **–est**.

Comparatives are used to **compare two things**. You can use sentences with than, or you can use a conjunction like but:

Examples: Sarah is shorter **than** Tom.

Sarah is tall, **but** Tom is taller.

Superlatives are used to compare **more than two things**. Superlative sentences usually use **the**, because there is only one superlative.

Examples: Tom is the tallest in the class.

Sarah is tall, and Mary is taller, but Tom is **the tallest.**

Comparatives and superlatives are forms of adjectives or adverbs that are used for comparing people or things.

POSITIVE	COMPARATIVE	SUPERLATIVE
Ugly	Uglier	Ugliest
Fast	Faster	Fastest
Beautiful	More beautiful	Most beautiful
Expensive	More expensive	Most expensive

If a group of words containing a subject and verb acts as an adjective, it is called an **Adjective Clause.**

Example: My sister, who is much younger than I am, is an Air Force pilot.

If an adjective clause is stripped of its subject and verb, the resulting modifier becomes an **Adjective Phrase:**

Example: She is the woman ~~who is~~ keeping her family in the poorhouse.

The word form of the positive is the adjectives or adverbs themselves. You should add **er** for the comparative degree and **est** for the superlative of the adjectives or adverbs of two or less syllables. For

71

those adjectives of two or more syllables and for adverbs ending in **ly, more** is used for the comparative and **most** for the superlative. There are some adjectives and adverbs that have irregular forms. Some of them are:

POSITIVE	COMPARATIVE	SUPERLATIVE
Good/well	Better	Best
Bad	Worse	Worst
Little	Less	Least
Many/Much/Some	More	Most
Far	Further	Furthest

Adverbs are often confused with adjectives. As noted in the **Building Sentences** section of this booklet, most adverbs tell: how, where, or when something is done. In other words, they describe the *manner, place,* or *time* of an action. Most adverbs end in *ly.* Most of these are created by adding ly to the adjective.

Examples: <u>Adjective</u>   <u>Adverb</u>

aggressive   aggressively

delightful	delightfully
hopeless	hopelessly
slow	slowly

She is an <u>aggressive </u>tennis player. (adjective)

She plays tennis <u>aggressively</u>. (adverb)

He is a <u>slow</u> walker.

He walks <u>slowly.</u>

However, this is NOT a reliable way to find out whether a word is an adverb or not, for two reasons: many adverbs do NOT end in -LY (some are the same as the adjective form), and many words which are NOT adverbs DO end in -LY (such as *kindly, friendly, elderly* and *lonely*, which are adjectives). Here are some examples of adverbs which are the same as adjectives:

Examples:	<u>Adjective</u>	<u>Adverb</u>
	Early	Early
	Fast	Fast
	Late	Late

"The **early** bird catches the worm." (adjective)

We are leaving **early** tomorrow morning. (adverb)

He is a **late** bloomer. (adjective)

We will get there **late**. (adverb)

The words **well** and **good** often cause challenges in how they are used. **Well** is an **adverb** and **good** is an **adjective**. However, the context of the sentence determines how each word is used.

Examples: Fredericka is **well** again. (adjective meaning "in good health")

Delonte´ is a **good** writer. (adjective describing writer)

Our team did a **good** job last night. (adjective describing job)

Our team did **well** last night. (adverb of manner)

The words **bad** and **badly** often cause challenges in usage. **Bad** is an **adjective** and **badly** is used as an **adverb**. The words **poor** and **poorly** cause similar challenges.

> Examples: Put all the **bad** oranges in that box. (adjective describing oranges)
>
> Juan thinks he played **badly** in the game. (adverb modifying played)

ANTECEDENTS AND APPOSITIVES

ANTECEDENT means going before, or preceding.

The antecedent is the word or group of words to which a pronouns refers or that the pronoun replaces.

> **Majesty** writes *her* poems in a notebook.
>
> The **boy** *who* ran the marathon is worn out.
>
> **Jasmine** and **Michael** are famous for *their* writing.

An **APPOSITIVE** is a noun, noun phrase, or noun clause which follows, usually next to, a noun or pronoun and renames or describes the noun or pronoun.

> My *student* **Diamond** works at the library after school.
>
> Her *brother* **Lamar** is not going to college now.
>
> Here comes the *assistant principal,* **Mr. Vann**.

An **APPOSITIVE PHRASE** is an appositive plus any words that modify the appositive. (In grammar, modify means to limit the meaning of. For Example, "old" modifies "man" in "old man.")

She is saving money to travel to *Charlotte*, **the largest city in North Carolina.**

Mr. Bull, **the history teacher,** is going to Bermuda for Christmas.

Anita, **Benita's twin sister,** does not work here.

DOUBLE NEGATIVES

A double negative is the nonstandard usage of two negatives used in the same sentence so that they cancel each other and create a positive. Two negatives make an affirmative or positive. Therefore, the use of double negatives is not wrong, especially when speaking, if they are intended to make a positive. For Example:

Wrong: I <u>don't</u> want <u>nothing</u> for my troubles.

This means something **is wanted** for the troubles.

Right: I don't want **anything** for my troubles.

This means **nothing** is wanted for the troubles.

Most negative words have positive forms. You can usually correct a double negative by using a positive form.

	<u>Negative</u>	<u>Positive</u>
Examples:	neither	either

78

never	ever
no	a, any
nobody	anybody
none	any
no one	any one
nothing	anything
nowhere	anywhere

Some subtle negative words commonly used:

hardly	scarcely	neither
barley	except	ever
merely	just	seldom

but (used as only)

WRITING

Writing is a process that involves a lot of trials and errors, but it is a process that can be mastered with persistence and careful thought about the exact message you want your reader to get. One of the essential things to think about when writing is that there might have to be several versions or iterations of a written piece before it is ready for your reader to read it. This is especially true for serious writings such as compositions, essays, or research papers. The essay probably is the primary written piece that most students will produce during their high school educational experience. While all essays are similar in structure, they serve different purposes, as outlined in the table on the following page. Novels, short stories, drama and poetry have unique characteristics and structures and will not be covered in this publication.

Choosing a Topic is an important aspect of a paper. The topic should be a statement, not a sentence, and should capture the essence of the message you want your reader to get from your paper. First, decide what you want to discuss in general. Then narrow your topic to make a more specific topic. Then, narrow that topic to several smaller topics. The result will be the scope of your paper. If the topic is too broad, the paper will probably result in general information. If the topic is too narrow, finding a way to write an effective paper is more challenging.

ESSAY TYPES

TYPE	EXPLANATION/PURPOSE
Argumentative	To win the reader over to your side or point of view of the argument. To show that you have a valid argument and to try to convince the reader to either adopt your position or to "agree to disagree."
Cause and Effect	To show how one thing leads to another, or that one cause can generate multiple effects.
Compare and Contrast	To take two subjects and show the similarities and differences between them.
Critical	To critique or review another work, usually one which is arts related (i. e. book, play, movie, painting). It is an objective analysis of the work, examining both its positive and negative aspects.
Descriptive	To give a description of an activity, an event or something. The essay can be subjective, personal beliefs and feelings, or objective, based only on the facts, and is meant to leave the reader with an impression.
Expository /Informational	To share information that is concise and clear. To expose the specific topic in a way that makes the information very clear to the reader.
Narrative /Personal	To get the writer to talk about herself or himself. In essence, it is a short story about the author's life.
Persuasive	To convince the reader to adopt your point of view; to take a specific course of action.
Reflective	To offer an evaluation of your feelings and findings from an experience, and what you learned from the experience.
Research	To share information that resulted from compiling, organizing and analyzing research and publishing the results as a research or term paper.

The writing process involves several critical steps: **Prewriting, Drafting, Revising, Editing and Presenting.**

Pre-writing is getting your thoughts down on paper. This can be done with free-writes (ideas and thoughts that come to mind), outlines or notes.

Drafting is putting your ideas and thoughts together sentence-by-sentence and paragraph-by-paragraph.

Revising is rewriting or rearranging sentences and paragraphs to make sense.

Editing is correcting grammar, punctuation, usage, etc.

Presenting is sharing your finished paper.

This process takes time and should not be rushed if you expect to do well on a paper. A good grasp of grammar, mechanics and usage of Standard English helps to advance the writing process. However, having something to say, which we all do, is critical to the success of a well-written piece. Any writing entails stringing together our words to make understandable sentences, then our sentences to create informative paragraphs, and then our paragraphs to make a complete and interesting composition, essay, or research paper. The series of sentences in a paragraph should be organized and coherent, and they all should be related to a single topic. Almost every piece of writing that is longer than a few sentences should be organized into paragraphs. Paragraphs show the reader where the subdivisions of a piece begin and end, and help the reader to understand the organization of the essay and to grasp its main points.

Most paragraphs in a composition or essay have a three-part structure—**introduction, body, and conclusion**. This structure in paragraphs can be identified, whether the paragraphs are comparing, contrasting, describing, narrating or analyzing information. Each part of the paragraph plays an important role in communicating the intended meaning to the reader.

Introduction: This section should include the **topic sentence** and any other sentences at the beginning of the paragraph that give background information about the subject. This section, especially the topic sentence, should also tell the reader that the writer has something important to explain or say and why. The topic sentence should be broad enough in scope to allow the remainder of the piece to provide the details. However, if a topic sentence is

83

too broad or general, the remainder of the paragraph will have to be either extremely long in order to give an adequate explanation of the idea, or it will have to contain nothing but more general statements. It should contain the controlling idea of the paper and point the direction the written piece will take. The topic sentence also advises the reader of the subject to be discussed and how the paragraphs will be sequenced to discuss it.

Body: This section follows the introduction and discusses the controlling idea, using analysis, arguments, examples, facts and other information to support what the writer is claiming in the introduction. This section of the essay typically includes at least three paragraphs. While all of them are different, they all are related to each other and provide additional information to complete the message the writer is intending to send.

Conclusion: This final section summarizes the connections between the information discussed in the body of the paragraph and the paragraph's controlling idea. It, in essence, is a summary of the entire composition, essay or research paper.

Effective writings include useful **transition words or statements** that connect throughout the written piece. These are very specific words that are used to emphasize the relationships between ideas and allow the writer to move smoothly from the introduction to the conclusion of each paragraph. They also help the reader to follow the writer's train of thought that might otherwise be missed or misunderstood. Included among them are words that:

Show addition: again, and, also, besides, equally important, first (second, etc.), further, furthermore, in addition, in the first place, moreover, next, too

Give examples: for example, for instance, in fact, specifically, that is, to illustrate

Compare: also, in the same manner, likewise, similarly

Contrast: although, and yet, at the same time, but, despite, even though, however, in contrast, in spite of, nevertheless, on the contrary, on the other hand, still, though, yet

Summarize or conclude: all in all, in conclusion, in other words, in short, in summary, on the whole, that is, therefore, to sum up

Show time: after, afterward, as, as long as, as soon as, at last, before, during, earlier, finally, formerly, immediately, later, meanwhile, next, since, shortly, subsequently, then, thereafter, until, when, while

Show place or direction: above, below, beyond, close, elsewhere, farther on, here, nearby, opposite, to the left (north, etc.)

Indicate logical relationship: accordingly, as a result, because, consequently, for this reason, hence, if, otherwise, since, so, then, therefore, thus

(Adapted from Diana Hacker, *A Writer's Reference*)
Examine how Dr. Stephen Jay Gould used transitions in a piece titled "Were Dinosaurs Dumb?" Pay attention to the capitalized words:

> I don't wish to deny that the flattened, minuscule head of the large-bodied "stegosaurus" houses little brain from our subjective, top-heavy perspective, BUT I do wish to assert that we should not expect more of the beast. FIRST OF ALL, large animals have relatively smaller brains than related, small animals. The correlation of brain size with body size among kindred animals (all reptiles, all mammals, FOR EXAMPLE) is remarkably regular. AS we move from small to large animals, from mice to elephants or small lizards to Komodo dragons, brain size increases, BUT not so fast as body size. IN OTHER WORDS, bodies grow faster than brains, AND large animals have low ratios of brain weight to body weight. IN FACT, brains grow only about two-thirds as fast as bodies. SINCE we have no reason to believe that large animals are consistently stupider than their smaller relatives, we must conclude that large animals require relatively less brain to do as well as smaller animals. IF we do not recognize this relationship, we are likely to underestimate the mental power of very large animals, dinosaurs in particular.

Sentence and paragraph coherence are essential to the effectiveness of a good piece of written material. Sentence coherence is present when each sentence flows smoothly into the next without obvious shifts or jumps in tone or thoughts. Paragraph coherence is present when one paragraph makes a smooth transition to another and makes the structure of ideas or arguments clear to the reader. You can establish coherence in a piece by employing several techniques: 1) Consistency in point of view, verb tense and number; 2) Use of parallel structures; and 3) Repeated use of key words or phrases.

Consistency in point of view, verb tense, and number is a subtle but important aspect of coherence. If you shift from the more personal "you" to the impersonal "one," from past to present tense, or from "a man" to "they," for example, you make your paragraph less coherent. Such inconsistencies can also confuse your reader and make your argument more difficult to follow.

Parallel structures are created by constructing two or more phrases or sentences that have the same grammatical structure or similar words (nouns, adjectives, etc), phrases (prepositional phrases, verbal phrases, etc.), or clauses (dependent, independent, etc). The application of **parallelism** in sentence construction improves writing style and readability. In addition, repeating a pattern in a series of consecutive sentences helps your reader see the connections between ideas. Parallel structures help the reader

87

see that the paragraph is organized as a set of examples of a general statement.

All of the following sentences are **unparallel**. See if you can determine what must be done to make them parallel:

1. He likes cooking, reading and to jog.
2. The dog ran across the yard, jumped over the fence and down the road he raced.
3. Thomas admires people with integrity and who have character.
4. The nurse took my blood pressure, temperature and I was weighed.

Repeated use of key words or phrases throughout the piece helps to re-enforce the importance of the writer's ideas or theory and to bind the paragraph together.

You may also integrate relevant **foreign expressions** or words into your writing. They often can say something succinctly that might take you many sentences to say. When these devices are used and placed appropriately and in the correct context in your writing, they can give your work a deeper level of appreciation and cast you as a credible and serious writer.

WRITING GUIDES AND BIBLIOGRAPHIES

A **style guide** or **style manual** is a set of standards for design and writing of documents, either for general use or for a specific publication or organization. Style guides are used when writing for the general public and for specialized audiences, such as students and scholars of the various academic disciplines, business and industry, government, journalism, law and medicine. Some style guides focus on graphic design and web sites covering such topics as typography and white space. Style guides focus on a publication's visual and technical aspects, prose style, best usage, grammar, punctuation, spelling, etc. They also describe how to cite references in the text of a document and in the bibliography. Listed below are some of the more popular or often-used style manuals:

- AAA (American Anthropological Association) Style

- APA (American Psychological Association) Style

- ASA (American Sociological Association) Style

- CSE (Council of Science Editors) Style

- CMS (*Chicago Manual of Style*)

- CGOS (*Columbia Guide to Online Style*)

- Harvard *Style Manual* (*HSM*)

- MLA (Modern Language Association) Style

- SWSM (*Skrunk and White Style Manual*)

- *Turabian Style Manual*

Many written pieces, especially research papers, require a **bibliography** that cites references that have been used. A bibliography is a list of sources of information on a given subject, period, etc., or of the literary works of a given author, publisher, etc. It is a list of the books, articles, etc., used or referred to by the author.

MLA (Modern Language Association) style is most commonly used to write papers and cite sources for high school research papers. The following information outlines how to cite references in the bibliography using the MLA style. Refer to the style guide or manual for guidance regarding including references within the text of a document.

Books with One Author—Last name, First name. *Title of Book.* Place of Publication: Publisher, Year of Publication.

- Books with one author—Gleick, James. *Chaos: Making a New Science.* New York: Penguin Books, 1987.

- Henley, Patricia. *The Hummingbird House.* Denver: MacMurray, 1999.

Books with More Than One Author—First author name is written last name first; subsequent author names are written first name, last name.

- Gillespie, Paula, and Neal Lerner. *The Allyn and Bacon Guide to Peer Tutoring.* Boston: Allyn, 2000.

An Author Who Has More Than One Book Cited—After the first listing of the author's name, use three hyphens and a period instead of the author's name. List books alphabetically by title.

- Brower, Wilbur L. *A Little Book of Big Principles.* Edgewood, MD: Duncan & Duncan, 1999.

- ---. *Me Teacher, Me...Please!—Observations about Parents, Students and Teachers, and the Teacher-Learner Process.* Comfort, NC: PwP Publishing, 2002.

An Anthology or Collection—List by editor or editors, followed by a comma and "ed." or, for multiple editors, "eds."

- Hill, Charles A. and Marguerite Helmers, eds. *Defining Visual Rhetorics.* Mahwah, NJ: Lawrence Erlbaum Associates, 2004.

- Peterson, Nancy J., ed. *Toni Morrison: Critical and Theoretical Approaches.* Baltimore: Johns Hopkins UP, 1997.

Book with No Author—List and alphabetize by the title of the book.

- *Encyclopedia of Indiana.* New York: Somerset, 1993.

An Article in a Newspaper or Magazine—Author(s). "Title of Article." *Title of Periodical* Day Month Year: pages.

An Article in a Newspaper or Magazine—When writing the date, list day before month; use a three-letter abbreviation of the month (e.g., Jan., Mar., Aug.). If there is more than one edition available for that date (as in an early and late edition of a newspaper), identify the edition following the date (e.g., 17 May 1987, late ed.).

- Poniewozik, James. "TV Makes a Too-Close Call." *Time* 20 Nov. 2000: 70-71.

- Trembacki, Paul. "Brees Hopes to Win Heisman for Team." *Purdue Exponent* 5 Dec. 2000: 20.

An Article in a Scholarly Journal—Author(s). "Title of Article." *Title of Journal* Volume. Issue (Year): pages.

Actual example:

- Bagchi, Alaknanda. "Conflicting Nationalisms: The voice of the Subaltern in Mahasweta Devi's Bashai Tudu." *Tulsa Studies in Women's Literature* 15.1 (1996): 41-50.

An Entire Web Site—Basic format:

Name of Site. Date of Posting/Revision. Name of institution/ organization affiliated with the site (sometimes found in copyright statements). Date you accessed the site <electronic address>.

- *The Purdue OWL Family of Sites.* 26 Aug. 2005. The Writing Lab and OWL at Purdue and Purdue University. 23 April 2006 <http://owl.english.purdue.edu/>.

- Felluga, Dino. *Guide to Literary and Critical Theory.* 28 Nov. 2003. Purdue University. 10 May 2006 <http://www.cla.purdue.edu/english/theory/>.

A Page on a Site—"Caret." *Wikipedia: The Free Encyclopedia.* 28 April 2006. 10 May 2006 <http://en.wikipedia.org/wiki/Caret>.

- "How to Make Vegetarian Chili." *eHow.com.* 10 May 2006 <http://www.ehow.com/how_10727_make-vegetarian-chili.html>.

- An Article in a Web Magazine—Author(s). "Title of Article." *Title of Online Publication.* Date of Publication. Date of Access <electronic address>.

Bernstein, Mark. "10 Tips on Writing The Living Web." *A List Apart: For People Who Make Websites.* No. 149 (16 Aug. 2002). 4 May 2006 <http://alistapart.com/articles/writeliving>.

An Article in a Database on CD-ROM—"World War II." *Encarta.* CD-ROM. Seattle: Microsoft, 1999.

93

A Personal Interview—Listed by the name of the person you interviewed.

- Adams, Mark. Personal Interview. 1 Dec. 2006.

- Broadcast TV or Radio Program—The Blessing Way." *The X-Files*. Fox. WXIA, Atlanta. 19 Jul. 1998.

Films and Movies—List films by their title, and include the name of the director, the film studio or distributor and its release year. If other information, like names of performers, is relevant to how the film is referred to in your paper, include that as well.

Recorded Movies—Include format names; "Videocassette" for VHS or Betamax, DVD for Digital Video Disc. Also list original release year after director, performers, etc.

- *Ed Wood*. Dir. Tim Burton. Perf. Johnny Depp, Martin Landau, Sarah Jessica Parker, Patricia Arquette. 1994. DVD. Touchstone, 2004.

Entire Albums—List by name of group or artist (individual artists are listed last name first). Label underlined or in italics, followed by label and year.

- Foo Fighters. *In Your Honor.* RCA, 2005.

- Waits, Tom. *Blue Valentine.* 1978. Elektra/Wea, 1990.

Individual Songs—Place the names of individual songs in quotation marks.
- Nirvana. "Smells Like Teen Spirit." *Nevermind.* Geffen, 1991.

94

COMMON MISTAKES AND MISUSED WORDS

COMMON MISTAKES AND MISUSED WORDS

INCORRECT	CORRECT
We was	We were
They was	They were
Who's	Whose
Whose	Who's
City State	City, State
Alot	A lot
There	Their
Their	There
Then	Than
Than	Then
Too/to	To/too
Hit the road	Began/Started our trip
I've took	I've taken
An hotel	A hotel
An male	A male
Came the greeted us	Came to greet us
Me and my family	My family and I
Me and some of my friends	Some of my friends and I
Fare	Fair
May be	Maybe
Wat	What
Two	Too
Lie	Lye
Lie	Lay, laid
Passed	Past
Waist	Waste
All ways	Always
All so	Also
Your	You're, yore
Its	It's
Could of	Could have
No	Know
All ready	Already
Any way	Anyway
Bye	By, buy, bi
Cite	Site, sight
Loose	Lose
Peace	Piece
Rain	Reign, rein
Rays	Raise, raze
Seen	Scene

95

Threw	Through
Weak	Week
Right	Write, rite, wright
Farther	Further
All together	Altogether
Principle	Principal
Break	Brake
Sense	Scents, cents
Accept	Except
Adopt	Adapt
Appraise	Apprise
Allusion	Illusion
Corps	Corpse
Discreet	Discrete
Foreword	Forward
Hanger	Hangar
Plain	Plane
Proceed	Precede
Roll	Role
Stationary	Stationery
Weather	Whether
Miner	Minor
New	Knew
Dessert	Desert
Their	They're
Want	Won't (contraction for will not)
Were	Where
Cheeper	Cheaper
Grate	Great
Wheather	Whether
In	And
Their	They're

Between vs. Among—Between—used for two people or two things. "The red house is between the white house and the yellow house."

Among—used for three or more people or things. "There was agreement among the three of them about where to go for vacation." "The pretty flower grew among the weeds."

Irregardless—This word, which is not in Standard English, is often mistakenly used for **regardless.**

IRREGULAR VERB FORMS

SIMPLE PRESENT, SIMPLE PAST AND PAST PARTICIPLE

SIMPLE PRESENT	SIMPLE PAST	PAST PARTICIPLE
arise	arose	arise
awake	awoke	awoken
be	was, were	been
bear	bore	borne
beat	beat	beaten or beat
become	became	become
begin	began	begun
bend	bent	bent
bet	bet	bet
bite	bit	bitten
bleed	bled	bled
blow	blew	blown
break	broke	broken
bring	brought	brought
build	built	built
burn	burned or burnt	burned or burnt
burst	burst	burst
buy	bought	bought
catch	caught	caught
choose	chose	chosen
cling	clung	clung
come	came	come
cost	cost	cost
creep	crept	crept
cut	cut	cut
deal	dealt	dealt
dig	dug	dug
dive	dived or dove	dived
do	did	done
draw	drew	drawn
dream	dreamed or dreamt	dreamed or dreamt
drink	drank	drunk
drive	drove	driven
eat	ate	eaten

fall	fell	fallen
feed	fed	fed
feel	felt	felt
fight	fought	fought
find	found	found
fit	fit, fitted	fit, fitted
flee	fled	fled
fling	flung	flung
fly	flew	flown
forbid	forbade or forbad	forbidden or forbad
forget	forgot	forgotten
forgive	forgave	forgiven
forgo	forwent	forgone
freeze	froze	frozen
get	got	gotten
give	gave	given
go	went	gone
grind	ground	ground
grow	grew	grown
hang	hung or hanged	hung or hanged
have	had	had
hear	heard	heard
hide	hid	hidden
hit	hit	hit
hold	held	held
hurt	hurt	hurt
keep	kept	kept
hurt	hurt	hurt
kneel	knelt or kneeled	knelt or kneeled
knit	knitted or knit	knitted or knit
know	knew	known
lay	laid	laid
lead	led	led
leap	leapt or leaped	leapt or leaped
leave	left	left
lend	lent	lent
let	let	let
lie (down)	lay	lain
light	lit or lighted	lit or lighted

lose	lost	lost
make	made	made
mean	meant	meant
meet	met	met
pay	paid	paid
prove	proved	proved or proven
put	put	put
quit	quit	quit
read	read	read
ride	rode	ridden
ring	rang	rung
rise	rose	risen
run	ran	run
saw	sawed	sawed or sawn
say	said	said
seek	sought	sought
sell	sold	sold
send	sent	sent
set	set	set
sew	sewed	sewn or sewed
shake	shook	shaken
shave	shaved	shaved or shaven
shear	sheared	sheared or shorn
shine	shone or shined	shone or shined
shoot	shot	shot
show	showed	shown or showed
shrink	shrank	shrunk
shut	shut	shut
sing	sang	sung
sink	sank	sunk
sit	sat	sat
slay	slew	slain
sleep	slept	slept
slide	slid	slid
sneak	sneaked or snuck	sneaked or snuck
speak	spoke	spoken
speed	sped	sped
spend	spent	spent
spill	spilled or spilt	spilled or spilt

spin	spun	spun
spit	spat or spit	spat or spit
split	split	split
spread	spread	spread
spring	sprang	sprung
stand	stood	stood
steal	stole	stolen
stick	stuck	stuck
sting	stung	stung
stink	stank or stunk	stunk
strew	strewed	strewn
strike	struck	struck or stricken
strive	strove or strived	striven or strived
swear	swore	sworn
sweep	swept	swept
swim	swam	swum
take	took	taken
teach	taught	taught
tear	tore	torn
tell	told	told
think	thought	thought
thrive	thrived or throve	thrived or thriven
throw	threw	thrown
undergo	underwent	undergone
understand	understood	understood
upset	upset	upset
wake	woke or waked	woken or waked
wear	wore	worn
weave	wove	woven
weep	wept	wept
win	won	won
withdraw	withdrew	withdrawn
wring	wrung	wrung
write	wrote	written
see	saw	seen

VERB CONJUGATIONS

SIMPLE TENSES indicates that an action is present, past or future, relative to the speaker or writer.

PRESENT	SINGULAR	PLURAL
1ST PERSON	I walk.	We walk.
2ND PERSON	You walk.	You walk
3RD PERSON	He/she/it walks.	They walk.

PAST	SINGULAR	PLURAL
1ST PERSON	I walked.	We walked.
2ND PERSON	You walked.	You walked.
3RD PERSON	He/she/it walked.	They walked.

FUTURE	SINGULAR	PLURAL
1ST PERSON	I will walk.	We will walk.
2ND PERSON	You will walk.	You will walk.
3RD PERSON	He/she/it will walk.	They will walk.

PERFECT TENSES indicate an action was or will be completed before another time or action.

Present Perfect	Singular
1st Person	I have eaten.
2nd Person	You have eaten.
3rd Person	He/she/it has eaten.

101

Past Perfect	Singular
1st Person	I had eaten.
2nd Person	You had eaten.
3rd Person	He/she/it had eaten.

Future Perfect	Singular
1st Person	I will have eaten.
2nd Person	You will have eaten.
3rd Person	He/she/it will have eaten.

PROGRESSIVE TENSES indicate continuing action.

Present Progressive	Singular
1st Person	I am dancing.
2nd Person	You are dancing.
3rd Person	He/she/it is dancing.

Past Progressive	Singular
1st Person	I was dancing.
2nd Person	You were dancing.
3rd Person	He/she/it was dancing.

Future Progressive	Singular
1st Person	I will be dancing.
2nd Person	You will be dancing.
3rd Person	He/she/it will be dancing.

The Fallacy of Student Failure

By Wilbur L. Brower

As an educational and business consultant and a school volunteer during the past fifteen years, I've been privileged to work closely with a number of students who have been labeled "a-risk" or "failures." During my involvement with these students, I have become keenly aware that they are neither at-risk nor failures because of who they are or what they currently cannot do. On the contrary, these students are put at-risk or they are failed because of what is not done with and for them in the educational system and through the teaching-learning process.

I believe, therefore, that the idea of student failure, in and of itself, is a fallacy. More specifically, I have perceived that this fallacy has evolved from three primary sources:

1) Parents and guardians who abdicate their responsibilities and leave the appropriate socialization and complete education of their children to the educational system.

2) Educators who set highfalutin, theoretical and impractical goals that emphasize testing and labeling students rather that educating them academically and cognitively, as well as

helping them to develop emotionally and socially; and

3) Politicians who have abused the educational system as a means to achieve political objectives.

First and foremost, parents and guardians put their children at-risk by assuming that the educational system is working in their best interest. When they fail to attend parent-teacher meeting and fail to be involved with the child's schooling experience, this has the appearance of, and often is interpreted as, the parents and guardians having no interest in their child's academic achievement, general well-being and future success. This apparent lack of interest is reinforced it the child enters the educational system without the basic learning and social skills expected of him or her.

If the child does not possess a reasonable degree of self-control and willingness to learn, he or she undoubtedly will be labeled and tracked as an under-achiever on the front end of the educational experience. If the parents or guardians discipline the child differently than the school or fail to correct inappropriate behaviors, the child will often experience behavior problems that cause him to be labeled "at-risk." Educators, in this case, are reluctant to impose discipline for fear of physical or verbal retaliation from the child, the parent and others in the school community. Furthermore, recent laws championing students' rights fail on the discipline front. Teachers who care enough to hold the line often find themselves the target of physical or verbal abuse charges.

Secondly, educators put students at-risk and ensure their failure by focusing on periodic tests and measurements rather than on progressive and continual learning. The unrelenting pressure for students to pass tests, at the expense of acquiring foundational knowledge and skills, will almost guarantee their failure in the future. The tests and measurements will overshadow true understanding and learning how to learn. Therefore, the trademark of the teaching-learning process should not be based solely on theoretical and impractical goals and objectives. Instead, the trademark of the educational system should be an open-door policy that accepts the student "as-is" and teaches her or him how to learn and how to think.

Highfalutin goals, objectives and mission statements have no practical value if little is actually done to ensure that all students participate in and benefit from the educational system in a constructive and wholesome manner. Goals, objectives and mission statements do not educate students. Educators and greater society must do it by helping students achieve their full potential, instead of labeling them at-risk or failure. Students defined as "at-risk" are those who are likely to leave school at any age without the academic, emotional, social and/or technical/vocational skills to lead productive lives.

I contend that these students are put at-risk and are allowed to become "failures" by the educational system. To eradicate this fallacy of student failure, educators must instill within these them self-confidence, self-motivation and self-worth. In addition, educators must focus on foundational knowledge and continual learning as means or ways to become more capable, rather than on "testing" just to gauge what they don't know and subsequently "labeling" students to decide what they might not be capable of learning. The remediation process used to help students who have less than successful academic outcomes is often a regurgitation of students' past learning experiences. Much needs to be done to create new experiences for these students that will: 1) allow them to learn according to their style of learning; 2) include experiential learning approaches implemented by teachers trained in this mode of learning; and 3 practical experiences that enrich the learning task, as a whole.

Thirdly, the fallacy of student failure has evolved from politicians who have abused the educational system as a means to achieve political objectives. Ironically, many of the politicians and individuals who control school boards are not educators and probably will spend time in a classroom only for a photo opportunity. The issue of who should be educated has been a perennial one, and the fervor surrounding it continues to escalate. The history of education in the United States, I believe, substantiates the fact that politicians have been vigilant in their appeasement of those who had the most economic and political clout and social standing regarding the education of their children, and have been less vigilant about or totally inattentive to those who had none. The history of education, coupled with the history of economic and voting rights, provides an interesting perspective on the politics of education.

I believe that it is incumbent upon politicians to end their role in student failure. They must face the reality that all students do not enter the educational system and the teacher-learner process at the same level. However, this should not deny some students the opportunity to acquire foundational knowledge and to develop basic skills that facilitate their continual learning, and the necessary funding and interventions for the knowledge and skills to be acquired.

Research reveals that student underachievement that is not

107

addressed properly puts them at-risk and ensures their failure. For example, research with third-grade students show that if....

- a poor child attends school comprised largely with other poor children;

- is reading a year behind the third grade;

- has been retained, or "left behind;"

- is from a low socio-economic background

- her or his chance of graduating from high school is near zero!

It is around the third-grade when students begin to see themselves as either learners or non-learners. Research also shows that eighty percent of all prison inmates are high school dropouts, and many have grown up in impoverished environments.

When students are achieving below grade level, funds must be made available to teach them how to achieve at or above grade level; they should not be merely told to achieve, but taught how to achieve. Many of the behaviors exhibited by students labeled "at-risk" emanate from their frustrations. They become frustrated due to subtle and overt messages that remind them that they cannot be smart because of their deficiencies. Students' negative behaviors often become defense mechanisms to protect their self-esteem and self-worth. Their deficiencies are not statements about what they are capable of becoming, but are statements about their current level of academic and intellectual development.

Rather than address what is causing the behaviors, it is often easier to label the student as the behaviors. If students are defined by their behaviors, then there is justification for making no significant changes. Therefore, few or no resources are allocated for this purpose. There is something wrong with a society when politician are allowed to declare that no resources are available to prevent or to intervene in a learner's at-risk behaviors, when some of the preventions and interventions cost only pennies or a few dollars. Successful learning programs, such as Sylvan Learning, are inaccessible to these students.

Conversely, the same politicians can easily find thousands of dollars to incarcerate that same at-risk learner many years for social transgressions for which effective preventions and interventions could have corrected. In fact, some states today are looking at student behaviors in the second and third grades and projecting how

109

many prisons will be needed to house or warehouse these children by the time they become young adults.

Investors today are encouraged to invest in companies that construct and operate prisons, with the expectation and promise that they will receive hefty returns on their investment. Ironically, these companies make up the "corrections industry." So, I have to ponder the question:

> Is there any public or private, non-monetary incentive to prevent and intervene in behaviors that are easily correctable?

I believe the "corrections industry" does little, if anything, to correct the behaviors, but they get billions of taxpayers' dollars annual for this purpose. There is no mistaking that there are many people imprisoned who deserve to be and should never be allowed freedom again. This includes young adults. But, there are far too many students who find themselves on the wrong track—the one headed for prison—and little is done to get them off. In fact, the inattention or negative attention they receive facilitates their ride to prison. Continually building prisons to accommodate prisons to them is not a viable solution for dealing with the problem.

One of the primary reasons for being in business is to move inventory or provide a service. The more inventory one moves or the move service one provides, the more money one expects to make. In the "corrections business," however, the more inventory one has the more money he or she will make. There is no incentive to get rid of inventory. This would suggest that there is little or no incentive to "rehabilitate" the inventory. Could this be a major factor contributing to the growing prison population?

If prison businesses were penalized for **not** rehabilitating their inventory, what affect might that have on the results of their rehabilitation efforts?

•••••••••••••••••••••••••••••••••••

I conclude, therefore, that student failure, to a great extent, is a combination of parental responsibility and the fallacious, though unintended, brainchild of educators and politicians. Students who are put at-risk and/or failed by parents, educators and politicians become a threat to society, and may ultimately cause society to be at-risk and/or become a failure. Talking about student failure and playing the "blame game" is time wasted, if no subsequent action is taken to ensure their success. This wasted time should be spent teaching students how to learn and showing them how to develop emotionally and socially. Students who are taught to grow and develop emotionally and socially often have difficulty developing academically. If all the emphasis is on their academic development, to the exclusion of their emotional and social development, it is almost certain that their academic development will be truncated; thus, they are put at-risk and failed by parents/guardians, educators and politicians.

We must do better as a civilized society.

From Me Teacher, Me....Please!—Observations about Parents, Students and Teachers, and the Teacher-Learner Process (2002) PWP Publishing

Parts of this essay were reproduced in its original form with a few additions and/or modifications. No matter how good a written piece appears to be, there are imperfections that become apparent each time you read it. This one is no exception.

FOREIGN EXPRESSIONS

AD HOC (AD hok) [Latin: for this purpose or specially] For a special purpose. *This is the third ad hoc committee appointed to complete the project.*

AMICUS CURIAE (ah-MEEK-us KOO-ree-ay) [Latin: friend of the court] A legal brief prepared in anticipation of a court decision by a person not directly involved on either side of the case but who has an interest in the outcome. *My office will file an amicus curiae with the appellate court tomorrow.*

BÊTE NOIRE (bet nwar) [French: black beast] Anything one avoids or dreads; a bugaboo. *For a solitary person, a party can be a bête noire.*

CARPE DIEM (CAR-pay DEE-um) [Latin: seize the day] (From the Odes of Horace)

COGITO ERGO SUM (CO-gih-tow AIR-go soom) [Latin: I think, therefore I am.] A brilliant insight by Descartes. But did he say it in Latin, as above, or in French? - "Je pense, dont je suis."

COMME IL FAUT (kom-eel-FOH) [French: as it should be; proper and fitting.]
Talking while I'm talking is not comme il faut.

CARTE BLANCHE (kart blawnsh) [French: a blank page] Full discretionary power. *With her enormous discretionary budget, she had carte blanche to plan the event.*

DÉJÀ VU (French: (day-zha voo) [French: already seen] The sense that one has already seen or done something in the past *Hearing of coming budget cuts, the manager had feelings of déjà vu.*

DE RIGUEUR (da-ree-GUR) [French: absolutely required by etiquette; mandatory]
Teachers' attendance at the graduation is de rigueur.

DEUS EX MACHINA (DAY-oose ex mah-KEEN-ah) [New Latin: God from machine] A literary device: when a plot becomes too complicated, the author introduces some element that no one would have anticipated. In Greek and Asian drama, a God literally descends (in a basket, from the ceiling) to straighten out a convoluted plot.

DRAMATIS PERSONAE (DRAM-a-tis per-SONE-eye) [New Latin: the cast of characters]

E.G. [Latin for *exempla gratia*] For example. Do not use interchangeably with i.e. (See *i.e.*) *Donate nonperishable items; e.g., canned goods.*

FAUX PAS (foe-pah) [French: false step] An offensive social act; an embarrassing slip. *He committed a faux pas by asking the principal if she were the custodian.*

GAUCHE (goash) [French: left, as in direction] Clumsy; lacking in tact or ease of manner. *Lessons in etiquette will prevent you from being gauche at President Barack Obama's Inaugural Dinner.*

HOI POLLOI (hoy polloy) [Greek: the many or "the common people"] The masses, the majority. *The billionaire did not purchase a box seat because he wanted to sit among hoi polloi.*

I.E. [Latin for *id est*] That is. Do not use interchangeably with *e.g.* (See *e.g.*) *Only original English texts are studied (i.e., those by authors from English-speaking countries).*

115

dialogue between two people. *The lawyers settled the dispute in a pre-trial tête à tête.*

VIS-À- VIS (veez a vee) [French: face to face] In relation to; compared to. *The position of the union vis-à- vis the administration is contentious.*

WUNDERKIND (WOON der kind) [German: child prodigy] *The wunderkind solved calculus problems at age five.*

XANTHIPPE (zan tippy) [Greek: Socrates' wife] A shrew. *Xanthippe issued orders all day long.*

YIN & YANG (yin and yang) [Chinese: dark and bright] Two opposite yet complementary forces that produce all that comes to be in the universe. *Yin is feminine and yielding while yang is masculine and assertive.*

ZEITGEIST (tsite giste) [German: time spirit] The spirit of the times. *In step with the Zeitgeist, the company promoted respect for diversity.*

IN FLAGRANTE DELICTO (in fla-GRONT-tay da-LEK-toe) [Medieval Latin: caught in the act; caught red handed (literally: while the thing was blazing)]
The congressman was seen in flagrante delicto with a congressional aide.

IN PROPRIA PERSONNA (in PRO pre a per SONAH) [Medieval Latin: in ones own person or character: PERSONALLY; especially without the assistance of an attorney.] *I will be in court in propria personna.*

JUNTA (hoon tah) [Spanish: joined] A military group or faction taking power after an overthrow. *The junta brought economic stability to the populace, but he did not bring political freedom.*

KITSCH (kitsh) [German: artifacts of low quality] Art or literature of cheap, tasteless, popular, sentimental quality. *Tourists often buy kitsch at souvenir stands.*

LAISSEZ-FAIRE (lessay fare) [French: let do] Policy of noninterference. By giving bailouts to *inductries, the government ended its laissez faire policy.*

MEA CULPA (maya kulpa) [Latin: my fault] An acknowledgment of one's guilt or responsibility. *The politician's sincere apology was the mea culpa the public was expecting.*

MIRABILE DICTU (meer-RAB-a-lah DICK-two) [Latin: astonishing or marvelous to say.] *Although soundly beaten in all nine rounds to date, he announced - mirabile dictu - that he would win the fight in the last round.*

NE PLUS ULTRA (neh ploos UUL-trah) [perfect; the very best Literally: "not more beyond"] *Winning the state champions hip is the ne plus ultra to which every school aspires.*

NON SEQUITUR (non SEEK witoor) [Latin: it does not follow] A statement that does not logically follow from what preceded it. *The answer "headache" was a non sequitur to my question, "What would you like to eat?"*

OMBUDSMAN (ohm budz men) [(Swedish: commissioner, agent] An official who looks into complaints by individuals against authorities. *An ombudsman resolved the senior citizen's tax abatement issue.*

PER [Latin: through, by means of] Use as per se, percent, per person but not as per your conversation. Use *according to. As per instructions, connect the white wire before you connect the red one.*

QUID PRO QUO (kwid pro kwo) [Latin: something for something] An action performed or a thing done in exchange for another.] *I did her a favor without exacting a quid pro quo.*

RAISON D'ÊTRE (rehzon detra) [French: reason to be] Reason for being. In modern use, it is to describe the main purpose for someone's life: to be a politician, a golfer, etc. *Volunteering was her raison d'etre.*

SINE QUA NON (SIN-nay qua non) [Latin: "without which, not" Something indispensable or absolutely necessary.] *Lifejackets are sine qua non on a ship.*

STATUS QUO (stat us kwo) [Latin: state in which] Existing state of affairs. *Never one to accept the status quo, he initiated major changes the same day he was sworn into office.*

TÊTE À TÊTE (tate a tate) [French: head to head] A private

REFERENCES

Brower, Wilbur L. *Me Teacher, Me....Please!—Observations about Parents, Students and Teachers, and the Teacher-Learner Process* Comfort, NC: PWP Publishing,   2000

Glencoe Grammar and Composition Handbook, High School 1 Columbus, OH: Glencoe/McGraw-Hill (2000).

Gould, S. J. (1978). "Were dinosaurs dumb?" *Natural History,* 87(5) (1978): 9-16.

Hacker, Diana, *A Writer's Reference.* Boston, MA: Bedford—St. Martins (2006).

Merriam-Webster's Manual for Writers & Editors—A clear, authoritative guide to effective writing and publishing. (1998). Springfield, MA: Merriam-Webster Inc. (1998)

ABOUT THE AUTHOR

Dr. Wilbur Brower is a graduate of North Carolina Public Schools. In addition to being a certified high school Business Education and English teacher, he is also a management and educational consultant and trainer. Dr. Brower is a former member of the U. S. Air Force and an executive with Bell Telephone Laboratories and AT&T, where he held numerous line and staff positions.

Dr. Brower earned an undergraduate degree in English Education, an MBA in Management and a Doctoral Degree in Business Administration, with a concentration in Human and Organizational Development. He also did post-graduate studies in Human Resources Planning and Management. He is the author of A Little Book Big Principles—Values and Virtues for a More Successful Life (1998) and Me Teacher, Me…Please! (2002). He also has been published in *Harvard Business Review* (Nov.-Dec. 1996) *Cultural Diversity at Work* (January, 1997) and *Vital Speeches of the Day* (Feb. 15, 2000). He is an avid reader, and he writes short stories and poems.

Made in the USA
Columbia, SC
16 July 2018